Dean Emeritus Roscoe Pound of the Law School of Harvard University is America's best-known legal scholar. Dean Pound, who will be 90 years old in October, 1960, was born and reared in Nebraska. He has been at Harvard for most of the last 50 years as law professor and as dean. Since his retirement he has served as visiting professor of law at the University of California, professor of law at the University of Calcutta, India, and adviser to the ministry of justice of the Republic of China. He has headed the most important national and international legal organizations and has been awarded 17 honorary degrees. His numerous published works have been translated into many foreign languages.

Law Finding
Through
Experience
and
Reason

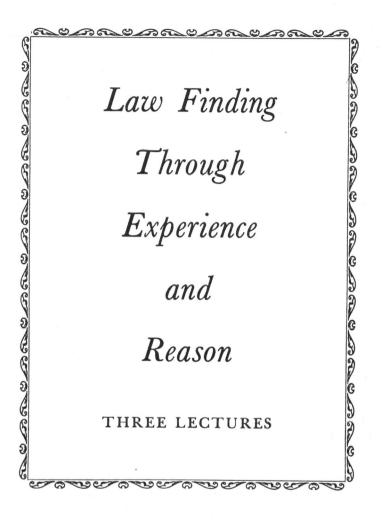

Law Finding Through Experience and Reason

THREE LECTURES

BY

ROSCOE POUND

UNIVERSITY OF GEORGIA PRESS

ATHENS

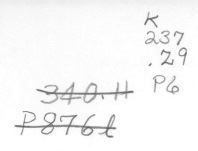

Contents

Foreword

THE UNIVERSITY OF GEORGIA IS THIS YEAR OBSERVING THE
centennial of its School of Law. Chartered by an Act of the
Georgia General Assembly in 1859, the School of Law is
the second of the schools and colleges of the University—
the Franklin College of Arts and Sciences being the oldest.

In June 1859, Joseph Henry Lumpkin, William Hope
Hull, and Thomas R. R. Cobb, acting under the sanction
of the Board of Trustees, issued a prospectus of the open-
ing session of a law school on October first as a part of The
University of Georgia. The School, the prospectus maintained, would be a blessing to the legal profession and the
community, the current custom of preparing for the Bar
by studying in the office of some lawyer being considered
inadequate.

"Believing that such a school is demanded," the prospectus continued, "we shall devote our energies to the
effort, which we will not abandon lightly. We expect
success only by deserving it. If we deserve it we shall
not fear obtaining it." The hopes of those who founded
the Law School have been largely realized in the careers
of thousands of lawyers who have studied at The University
of Georgia School of Law. Alumni of the School have
rendered distinguished service in the professional, political,
and cultural life of the State and Nation. As the Law

School enters upon another century, students and faculty pledge their best efforts toward carrying on the work begun by the founders.

To inaugurate our Centennial Celebration, we of the Law School desired to bring to the University campus one who by his scholarship and accomplishments had greatly contributed to the orderly development of the law and to a more effective administration of justice among our people. We felt that there was no one in America, or perhaps the world, better qualified or who would be heard with greater interest than Dean Emeritus Roscoe Pound of the Harvard Law School. The visit of Dean Pound was one of the most significant events of our Centennial Year. Now in his ninetieth year, he delivered three lectures dealing with the science of law, a subject to which he has devoted seventy years as a lawyer, judge, author, and law teacher.

It is with much pleasure that the University publishes and makes available these lectures in book form under the title *Law Finding Through Experience and Reason.*

J. ALTON HOSCH
Dean, School of Law
University of Georgia

Preface

IN AMERICA WE HAVE INHERITED AND DEVELOPED THE English faith in doing all things according to law. Moreover, as part of that inheritance, we have thought of law, not as something made, expressing will, but as something found, expressing reason. But common-law thinking has not taken place *in vacuo.* The common-law judges have been practical lawyers charged with a task of deciding actual controversies, not merely or even primarily of laying down universal pronouncements of eternal reason. They have had a task of applying reason to specific items of experience and thus reaching starting points for reasoning as experience has raised new problems.

Yet reasoning is not reason. It employs reason but, as experience has shown abundantly, does not always employ it reasonably. If it sometimes appears that the common law overemphasizes experience, it appears at times that the philosophical civilian overstresses what he takes to be the abstract eternal.

As we move, as we seem to be doing, toward a law of the world that is to bring us to world peace, it may be that we shall learn a just balance between making law *sub specie aeternitatis* and finding it through correction of our pictures of it as drawn to the experience of the past.

ROSCOE POUND

Harvard Law School
6 April 1960

ONE

Law Making and Law Finding

THERE ARE THREE SENSES IN WHICH THE TERM "LAW" IN English is commonly used. First, it is used to mean a regime of ordering society. Second, it is used to mean a body of precepts by which the regime is or is sought to be carried on so as to achieve justice. Third, it is used to mean an aggregate of precepts constraining conduct by which an ordered society is to be brought about. I shall call the first "the legal order." In French it is called *ordre juridique,* in German, *Rechtsordnung.* The second is in Latin *ius* and the third *lex.* In English it is called law, and in English the third, thought of as a body of rules, is thought of in terms of the several precepts and is spoken of as "rules of law" or "laws."

In the science of law we must make a careful distinction between the second and the third of these three meanings —between law and a law, between *the* law and *a* law, or in other words, between Law and Laws.

Law is a body of ideals, principles, and precepts for the adjustment of the relations of human beings and the ordering of their conduct in society. Law seeks to guide decision as laws seek to constrain action. Law is needed to achieve and maintain justice. Laws are needed to keep the peace—to maintain order. Law is experience developed by reason and corrected by further experience. Its

immediate task is the administration of justice; the at-
tainment of full and equal justice to all. The task of laws
is one of policing, of maintaining the surface of order.

Law is found; Laws are made. Law is governed by principles, starting points for reasoned decision, found by application of reason to experience and corrected by experience as the process of development of society goes on.
It deals with general conditions and situations, and seeks
to deal with them in universal rather than local terms.
When there are local conditions and situations rules become necessary. But a rule may express a locally applicable
principle. Although rules frequently are arbitrary, they
are not so always of necessity. Rules are prescribed by
sovereign political authority. Principles may be given
authority by adoption by sovereign political authority.
But the binding force of principles is moral; it may have
political backing but it is not primarily political. Rules
are made by legislative organs of the state—legislatures or
bodies or persons given rule-making power by constituted
authority.

The analytical theory, generally taught in England and
in the United States in the last half of the nineteenth
century and still not without adherents, is one of a law,
or perhaps more accurately of *the* law in terms of *a* law.
It proceeds in the pattern of the policing of the city-state
of antiquity, treating of law as a body of police regulations
of a small town in the rural pastoral or agricultural society of the beginnings. The historical theory, which developed in Continental Europe in the nineteenth century
and came more and more to prevail in England and in
the United States in the last quarter of the nineteenth and
earlier part of the present century, was in some ways more
metaphysical than historical. It grew out of a metaphysical
version of history. History was held to be a story of the
process of self-realization of an idea of individual freedom.

It belonged to the era of faith in the fullest and freest self-realization of the individual taken to be the purpose of human existence. It belonged to a time when it was assumed there was endless room for individual full and free self-assertion. There were undiscovered lands, unexplored regions, vast unoccupied public domain, plenty of room beyond the horizon to which the restless could move and find full outlet for their activity. But such is not the world in which the precepts of law are to be applied today. Today we must be thinking not of free self-control nor of full imposed control by a political sovereign, but of social control by the pressure of so many of our fellow men in an increasingly crowded world. This pressure, exerted both consciously through organized effort and social and political institutions, and subconsciously through their mere presence, is presupposed by the legal order.

Confused thinking about law and laws is promoted by a deficiency in the vocabulary of the Anglo-American lawyer. This deficiency stands in the way of recognizing the fundamental distinction of which I have been speaking and makes plausible a proposition that law is no more than an aggregate of laws. It has been seen that we have to do with three ideas. For the three ideas Latin has two words, *ius* and *lex*. In the modern languages, except English, there are likewise two words. In the Romance languages the Latin *ius,* law (but also *a* right as well as law because it is morally right) is replaced by a word derived from *directum*—straight, that is, law because it is straight in contrast to the crooked. So much for *the* law. *A* law, a rule of law, is represented by words derived from the Latin *lex.* So we have in French *droit* and *loi*, in Italian *diritto* and *legge*, in Spanish *derecho* and *ley*. In German also there are two words, *Recht*, both straight and right, and *Gesetz*, what is set down or prescribed and so *a* law. In Anglo-Saxon the word which became law in English is *lagu,* a word in the *lex* line rather than the *ius* line, which was used for the codified rules of Anglo-Saxon kings. Our word "right" did not get away from a purely moral sense. But the Scotch jurists have used the word as the equivalent of *ius* in books on jurisprudence and philosophy of law. As their law was the modern Roman law, taken over from the Continent in the sixteenth and seventeenth centuries, and the books they read were those of the civil law, this was natural.

Exigencies of the dictionary often govern reasoning and reasoning often stands for reason. Perhaps the dictionary had much to do with the dogma of the analytical jurists that law was a body of commands of the sovereign.

What we have to bear in mind is that law has to govern life and that the essence of life is growth and change.

In establishing an ordered society men have used two fundamental ideas, one moral, an idea taken from ethics, and the other political, an idea taken from political science. From the one we develop the idea of reasoned adjustment of relations and ordering of conduct in accord with principles. From the other we develop the idea of sanctioned rules imposed and enforced by a sovereign political authority. The one gives us law. The other gives us rules of law or laws. Rules call for a sovereign political authority. Principles of law call for judges, as in Anglo-American law, or jurists and law-teachers, as in Roman law and on the whole in the civil or modern Roman law, who find them through development of experience by reason.

On the whole in Continental Europe the idea of law rather than of laws, stress on the ethical rather than on the political side of administration of justice, has led to theories in terms of law. In England and America political revolutions in the seventeenth and eighteenth centuries, rise of the idea of the sovereignty of the self-governing people, led to stress upon the political side of the legal order, and so to thinking in terms of rules imposed by a sovereign—of laws rather than of law. In the nineteenth century, philosophy of history led to another way of thinking. Contact of exclusively ethical and exclusively political thought as to the nature of law with a metaphysical doctrine which taught the inherent power of an idea to realize itself and had much vogue for a time, led to a historical-philosophical theory of law as developed custom formulated by jurists and law teachers or discovered and given authoritative form by judges.

The problem which the legal order presents to the science of law is brought out in the dramatic ceremony of bringing an action at law *(legis actio)* which obtained in Rome down to the second century of our era. The plaintiff having summoned the defendant and both being in court, the two acted a street fight, and the judicial magistrate called out *"mitteto ambo"* (let go, both of you). Then each stated his case and the magistrate said, "Titius iudex esto" (Let Titius be judge). The case then went to the appointed person to be adjudged.

By what was Titius to judge? Was it to be the judge's individual sense of justice? Or the settled and recognized customs of the community? Or the customary way of deciding such cases as handed down from those who had judged in the past? If the last, was it to be as ascertained and expounded by a wise and learned custodian of custom? Or as expounded by learned commentators in books of more or less authority? Or as prescribed by a recognized custodian of the recorded course of decision?

In contrast it might be that Titius was to apply a rule laid down for such cases by rule-making authority. But the primitive codes, while going into infinite detail as to the penalties to be imposed and for what, seldom furnish much guidance for other than questions of policing.

Moreover, as we study the development of the judicial

process we must recognize the role of ideals of right and justice in giving shape to experience and to its development by reason.

As between the analytical conception of a body of rules formulated and put in force by an all-powerful, all-wise sovereign lawmaker—postulating, I suppose, that Justinian and Napoleon, who were politically all-powerful in their day, may claim credit for the wisdom of those who compiled the codes that bear their names—as between this and the conception of the nineteenth-century historical jurists that all lawmaking is *ex post facto* formulation of what had developed in the customary conduct of a people, the historical doctrine is much nearer the truth. Where the historical jurists spoke of custom, we now speak of experience of adjudication and qualify it as developed by reason.

The theory of law as something made by a legislative lawmaking organ of a politically organized society is a theory derived from the medieval commentators on the Corpus Juris, the compilation of Roman law under the auspices of and enacted by the emperor Justinian in the sixth century A.D. But what Justinian really did was to give legislative form and authority to what had been wrought by the Roman jurisconsults—professional legal advisors. Their opinions given to the judges by way of advice as to the law, were made into text books in the classical period of Roman law, the second to the fourth century A.D.

In fact the codes in the Civil Law world today are but enactments of what had been worked out in a course of teaching and text-writing by the great jurists and text-writers of the eighteenth and nineteenth centuries.

The idea of law as made, of the law-giver typified by Moses, "that shepherd who first taught the chosen seed how heaven and earth rose out of chaos," or, on the other hand, of decision as something given by inspiration, as in case of the saint-king who judged his people under the oak at Vincennes, overestimates the role of rule on the one hand, and that of inspiration on the other. What we must keep in mind is experience and reason. Experience teaches decisions that prove to satisfy demands of justice. Reason shapes and orders and develops decisions to ideals of justice and so into principles of law. I repeat: We must not underestimate the role of ideals in the development of the law.

Ideal gets its name from a Greek word meaning picture. An ideal of a thing is a picture of it to which we fit our conception of it as we think it is or ought to be. The ideals of the social order, however, which become authoritative guides to determination of controversies and ordering of conduct, are not photographs or photographically retouched drawings of the social order of the time and place. They are largely pictures of a social order of the past, drawn to it at its best, undergoing retouching as to details in order to fit exigencies of the present. Ideals of law and ideals of principles and rules of law, are pictures made to conform to an ethical-philosophical juristic picture of the legal order, intended to guide judges and legislators and administrative agencies toward making the means afforded by the legal order achieve its postulated ends.

Understanding and exposition of the ideal element in law, and of law as guided in its development by ideals, is the task of philosophy of law. Law had its beginnings as organized social control in the city-state of antiquity which grew out of the kin-group or groups of closely associated kindreds in the small town of the rural pastoral or agricultural society. Beginnings of thinking about law are to be seen in the classification of laws made by Hippodamus (middle of the fifth century B. C.) and quoted by Aristotle in his *Politics,* a book which has a large place in the devel-

opment of political science and of law. Hippodamus, we
are told, maintained that there were three subjects of law
suits, namely, to recover a penalty for insult, or for injury
to person or property, or for homicide, i.e., to buy off
the vengeance of the kin of the deceased. Law had got no
further than a systematized policing by imposition of penalties to be sued for in order to prevent war between kin-
groups and maintain the peace. In the fourth century B. C.
Plato and Aristotle are no longer writing merely of policing and of recovery of penalties to buy off vengeance and
obviate private war. Plato's *Republic* and Aristotle's *Politics* have from the beginning had a strong influence upon
political and juristic thought. Their picture of an ideal
city-state, an ideal Athens or Sparta, was the model of the
medieval academic picture of "the empire," a picture of
a universal state, ruled by universal law, which has been
received in the half of the modern world which adheres
to the civil or modern Roman law and is a strong element
in legal thinking everywhere. But there was nothing universal about the Greek city-state, and the medieval universal law of the postulated empire or universal state, working with the postulated universal church, was challenged
and lost much of its force with the rise of nationalism in
the seventeenth century.

Along with the superseding of the universal by the national idea went an insistence upon the individual human
being as the true and exclusive concern of both legal and
political philosophy. This is the dominant political and
legal philosophical dogma of the nineteenth century. But
before passing on to the beginnings of a revival of the
universal idea today, it will be worth while to look at the
stages of development of law from the time of the city-state.

Between the time of Hippodamus and the time of an
impending atomic age, which is variously held to portend
continued development along a settled continuous line

from the beginning or a wholly new start, we may distinguish four stages. I have been in the habit of calling them: The stage of the strict law, the stage of equity and natural law, the stage of maturity of law, and the stage of socialization of law.

In the stage of the strict law a legal order is definitely differentiated from other modes of social control, and law comes increasingly to be the paramount agency. When men come to appeal primarily and ultimately to organized society to redress wrongs done them, the body of precepts determining the cases in which their claim will be taken up and given effect has the result of defining interests or rights which the legal order recognizes and secures. Thus a body of procedural rules, leading to a system of remedies and formal procedure in order to obtain them, supersedes the tariff of compositions by which kin-organized society sought to maintain the peace. The characteristics of this stage of development of the law are: Formalism, reliance upon form and refusal to look beyond or behind it; rigidity and immutability—its rules (for it does not know principles) are not adaptable to conditions and circumstances; extreme insistence that everyone look out for himself; complete refusal to take account of the moral aspects of situations or transactions (as Dean Ames put it, the strict law is not immoral, but is unmoral); and arbitrary restriction of legal personality. In the strict law only legal persons have recognized rights and duties, and the class of legal persons is narrowly and arbitrarily limited.

While long outgrown, the strict law was a radical step forward from what has been spoken of usually as primitive law, but was in reality not law at all. The strict law advanced from the bare idea of keeping the peace to a general purpose of what we may call the general security. For the crude idea of composition—a compulsory buying off of vengeance in order to avoid private war—the strict law substituted the idea of legal remedies. From the vague idea of peaceable ordering of the community the strict law has developed the ideas of certainty and uniformity in that ordering and of rule and form as means of obtaining them.

To a succeeding stage of legal development, a stage of liberalization, Sir Henry Maine gave the very appropriate name of Equity and Natural Law. In Roman law, while its beginnings may be seen as far back as the second Punic War (middle of the second century B.C.) it is especially the period of the great jurists from Augustus (end of the first century B.C.) to the end of the first quarter of the third century A.D. In the common-law system it is the age of the rise of the Court of Chancery and development of equity and the rise and absorption of the law merchant— substantially the seventeenth and eighteenth centuries. In the Civil Law system of Continental Europe, it is represented by the period of what is called the Law-of-Nature school of jurists—the seventeenth and eighteenth centuries.

As I have put it elsewhere, the watchword of the strict law was certainty; the watchword of the stage of equity and natural law is some word or phrase of ethical import such as *aequum et bonum,* or good conscience, or natural law. Where the strict law insisted on uniformity, forms, remedies and rules, equity and natural law insisted on good morals, justice in the ethical sense, duties, and reasoned principles. The capital ideas of this stage are: Identification of law with morals, the conception of duty and attempt to make all moral duties into legal duties, and reliance upon reason rather than upon arbitrary rule to eliminate the personal element in the administration of justice.

Four enduring ideas of the first importance are developed in this stage: (1) That legal personality should extend to all human beings; (2) that law is to look to substance rather than to form; (3) that men are to act in good faith—that justice demands that well-founded expectations which one has created shall not be disappointed; and (4) that one person shall not be unjustly enriched at the expense of another.

But the attempt in this stage of development to make law coincide with morals led for a time to the attempt to make legal duties out of moral duties not tangible enough to be made effective by the machinery of the legal order. Also the attempt to identify law and morals gave too wide a scope to judicial discretion. Rules of law are of general and absolute application, whereas moral precepts must be applied according to circumstances and individuals. In this stage the tendency of equity is to make the administration of justice too personal and too uncertain. As Selden said of the equity of the sixteenth-century chancellors, it was "a roguish thing" the measure of which might as well be the length of the chancellor's foot as that of his conscience. This was corrected in the succeeding stage. But distrust of judicial discretion was carried too far for a time and today it is allowed wider scope.

In time there comes to be a process of stiffening in the legal order which leads to a fourth stage of development— the one in which my generation of lawyers was brought up. In comparison with the foregoing stage it is one of maturity. Perhaps each stage has in its own day thought of itself as final. At any rate, the nineteenth century was confident of having attained political and legal maturity. However this may be, a well marked stage of legal development was reached in the ancient world in the maturity of Roman law and again in the modern world in the nineteenth century, following in each case one of equity and natural law. On the fall of the Roman empire an era of strict law supervened in Europe and prevailed until humanist study of Roman law in the universities and economic and political progress brought about an era of equity and natural law, very marked both on the Continent and in England. This was succeeded in the nineteenth century by a stage of legal development which has been accounted one *par excellence* of legal maturity.

In this stage of matured legal system the watchwords are equality and security. Equality includes equal operation of legal precepts and equal opportunity to exercise one's faculties and employ one's substance—both a legal and an economic idea. Also the idea of security is twofold: that everyone is to be secured in his rights against aggression by òthers and that others are to be permitted to acquire from him only through his will that they do so or through his breach of precepts of law designed to secure others in like interests.

The characteristic institutions in this stage are property and contract. Its permanent contribution is perhaps thorough working out of the idea of individual interests.

In 1891, Jhering noted the beginnings of a tendency to depart from ideas which had governed the maturity of law. As he put it there was "formerly high valuing of property, lower valuing of the person; now lower valuing of property, higher valuing of the person." There was, he said, weakening of the sense of property, strengthening of the feeling of the moral and legal worth of the individual man. Today this has been becoming more marked. The maturity of law seeks to secure individuals in the advantages given them by their station in the world and to enable them to use those advantages as freely as may be compatible with like free exercise of their faculties and use of their advantages by others. Hence the maturity of law reverts in some measure to the ideas of the strict law and brings about once more a degree of opposition between law and morals. Neglect of the moral worth of the individual man through the insistence upon property and contract has increasingly been leading to absorption into the law of ideas developed in the social sciences.

At least ten significant developments in American law, and there are parallel developments in Europe, require notice. To go into them fully would require a series of lectures. I can only indicate an outline. Summarily stated they are: (1) Limitations on the use of property—as the French put it, prevention of the abusive exercise of rights; (2) limitations on freedom of contract—requirement of standard clauses and prescribing of standard contracts; (3) limitations on the *jus disponendi* of an owner, going back some way in America in homestead laws; (4) limitations upon the power of a creditor or an injured person to obtain satisfaction, notable today in Europe as well as in America; (5) development of liability without fault, a doctrine that reparation of injuries involved in the conduct of enterprises which in experience involve injuries to the person in their operation, shall be borne by the enterprise and passed on to the public as part of the cost of the product; (6) insistence upon the interest of society with respect to dependents; (7) an increasing tendency to hold that public funds should respond for injuries to individuals by public agencies; (8) reading of reasonableness into the obligation of contracts, for example, a developing doctrine of frustration; (9) increasing recognition of groups and associations as legal units, not limiting recognition to historical organizations and business and industrial devices on their analogy; and (10) an increasing tendency to relax the rules as to trespassers.

Interpretation of these changes seems to portend a stage of legal development to which I have been giving the name of the Socialization of Law. It is quite possible that we have already gone some little way toward such a fourth stage—call it what you like, since the word "social" frightens many today.

May I be allowed an essay at prophecy and suggest to what it may lead? Perhaps the most significant feature of development of law today is giving up of the extreme localism of the American lawyer of the last century. What Beseler called Kleinstaatismus, or, as I translate it, Mainstreetism, a characteristic of Germanic law, as compared with the universalism of Roman thinking, came to us with our Germanic common law. So with us there was long a cult of local law. The law of the time and place was thought to have an all-sufficient basis in local political sovereignty. There has been a notable change. The world has been increasingly unified commercially. Air transportation has annihilated distances and commercial transactions have always crossed political boundaries. Such transactions are coming to be world wide. The uniform commercial laws of today bear witness to a breakdown of the cult of local law.

Undoubtedly there must and will always be a certain amount of local law to meet special local conditions and circumstances. But there is not a little to indicate that working out a theory of local legislation and administration in a unified world may be the chief task of the jurists of tomorrow. What we shall have to do is to get rid of the idea that law, as distinguished from laws, is a body of commands of a political sovereign and that a politically organized world-state is a necessary prerequisite of a law of the world.

So much for the present status of development of the law. A chief agency in this development has been philosophy, since, if law is experience developed by reason, while history shows us the course of experience, philosophy shows the course of reason.

How has philosophy of law developed in the course of legal development and what is its present status?

What attracted the attention of Greek philosophers of the fifth and fourth centuries B.C. was adjustment of the strict law to the ethical and political principles they were busied in working out. A strict law had grown out of the primitive stage. There were codified rules on the model of which it was said that the Twelve Tables, the foundation of the Roman strict law, had been framed. These enacted rules governed the administration of justice in the Greek city-state. But the philosophers saw the distinction between the hard and fast rules laid down in the codes and the moral precepts—let us say, ethical principles —they were discussing. As they put it, there was a fundamental political distinction between the just by nature and the just by enactment. Enactment might succeed in formulating what was just by nature. But what was enacted would gain its morally binding force from its intrinsic or natural justice, not from its formal enactment.

In the hands of Roman lawyers of the classical era this idea of what was just by nature became controlling. It called for principles rather than for rules. Applied to the experience of decision of actual controversies by judges, who were advised as to applicable precepts by the jurists, this brought together the two elements, experience and reason, which make up law as distinguished from laws.

The schools or sects of jurists which have guided the development of law as we now know it, grew out of academic or professional teaching of law since the revival of study of Roman law in the Italian universities in the twelfth century. Medieval academic juristic theory presupposed continuity of the empire. The German-Roman empire was taken to be the empire of Augustus and Constantine and Justinian. Indeed this was a phase of the medieval academic dream of universality, which may now at long range prove to have been prophetic. There was held to be a universal civil law of Christendom, a law of the universal church, the canon law, a universal sea law, a universal law merchant, and universal customs of chivalry. The ideas of the civil law, the sea law, and the law merchant have proved fruitful for the law of today.

Law teaching in the medieval universities began with text-by-text interpretation of the codified Roman law of Justinian. Later the simple method which put system into each text was followed by a highly complicated one, based on formal logic and the scholastic philosophy, which put system into subjects rather than texts. It remained for the philosophers of the revival of learning to seek to put system into the law as a whole.

At the revival of learning the Humanists began the scientific study of law as it is carried on in the modern world. The founder, Andrea Alciati (Alciatus), an Italian teacher of law, who taught later at Bourges in France, weighed and discussed reasons instead of merely counting texts. His successors Cujaccius (Jacques Cujas, 1522-1590), a pupil of Alciatus, and Donellus (Doneau, 1527-1591), teacher at Bourges, are called the French School. Cujaccius is the pioneer of legal history and Donellus the pioneer of systematic classification of law as a whole. Back in the thirteenth century the scholastic philosophers had been considering the theological-philosophical bases of law and legal institutions. Philosophy of law, as we understand it today, in a sense begins with St. Thomas Aquinas (1225-1274). But by the fore part of the seventeenth century the academic theory of continuity of the empire broke down. Jurisprudence was emancipated from theology and law was emancipated from Justinian.

What marks the turning point to the science of law as we think of it today is the great work of Hugo Grotius (De Groot, 1583-1645), whose treatise on the Law of War and Peace was published in 1625. Following him came the Eighteenth Century Law of Nature School of jurists the influence of which, through Blackstone, is still felt in the science of law in America.

As I have summarized the matter elsewhere: The thirteenth century put theological philosophy behind law to sustain authority. The sixteenth and seventeenth centuries divorced philosophy of law from theology and divorced law (not laws) from authority. The nineteenth century divorced legal philosophy from political philosophy and set jurisprudence off definitely as a separate science. The twentieth century seeks to unite jurisprudence with the other social sciences through some form of social philosophy.

In the nineteenth century three distinct approaches to law led for a time to the setting off of three distinct schools of jurists. Putting them in order of time, they were historical, metaphysical, and analytical. Each of them, however, had a basic philosophy of law. The historical school held to a philosophy of history. Its founder and leader was Friedrich Carl von Savigny (1779-1861), professor at Berlin. It held that law was a necessary result of the whole history of a people. It was not something which speculation could bring forth full fledged from the head of a jurist or legislation could bring forth by an arbitrary fiat. In other words, it put stress on the experience element in law. Later, in revolt from the analytical jurisprudence, which had become dominant in the English-speaking world, came the English historical school of which the leader and chief exponent was Sir Henry Maine, professor at Oxford. On the basis of his experience as a legal adviser in India and his teaching of Roman law he established a comparative historical science of law. A purely philosophical method was employed during the nineteenth century by the metaphysical school. This school had its eye upon the reason element in law. Its founder was Immanuel Kant (1724-1804), who has held a commanding position in philosophy of law ever since his metaphysical foundations of the theory of law was published in 1797 (2d ed. 1798). He sought to work out an ideal body of principles from some fundamental idea of justice. Later the historical and the metaphysical schools substantially merged in Continental Europe.

While in Continental Europe and in Scotland revolt from the then dominant law-of-nature school kept to the ethical direction—the relation of jurisprudence to ethics, given to it in the beginning by the scholastic jurists of the thirteenth century—in England the revolt which came later took the political direction of the relation of jurisprudence to the science of politics. The forerunner was Jeremy Bentham (1748-1832), the pioneer of law reform and particularly of the reform of legal procedure which was achieved in England in 1873, had a promising beginning in New York in 1849, and has gone far in the United States since 1912.

Bentham was a utilitarian, and his zeal for practical results led him to look to the legislature for the far-reaching improvements in the administration of justice which he saw were much needed. John Austin (1790-1850), who taught jurisprudence at the University of London from 1826 to 1832, was a zealous utilitarian and attributes to Bentham the basis of the analytical jurisprudence which he founded. But it broke with philosophy. Instead of trying to deduce a universal system of law from the nature of man or to deduce an ideal body of legal precepts from some metaphysically ascertained starting point, Austin sought to take legal precepts as they were, to analyze the precepts and institutions as they actually existed, and to get in this way the materials for a universal science of law.

In truth, both the analytical and the historical jurists in

the last century set up, as one might say, systems of natural law of their own. Each assumed to find universal principles on which all law must rest. One found them by comparative analysis of precepts and institutions and doctrines of English and Roman law. The other found them by historical study of Roman and Germanic law. Analytical jurisprudence is still strong in England and, although threatened seriously by the English historical jurisprudence at the beginning of the present century, has still not a few adherents in the United States.

At the end of the nineteenth century the historical school, which had prevailed in Continental Europe, gave way. Two schools grew up and a new method developed which has led to a formative school of jurists with a distinct method of study of the legal order and in particular of the process of adjudication. Thus we have today two types of social philosophical school and a sociological school, and a method of economic interpretation which has been chiefly urged and developed by a neo-realist school.

Today we look at the methods of jurisprudence functionally. We ask what consequences have followed from pursuit of them—how far have they enabled the law to achieve its ends or interfered with achieving them. Looked at in this way, it is seen that the analytical method, as the one method of jurisprudence, has had two bad consequences: It led to what is called a jurisprudence of conceptions, in which new situations of fact were always to be met by deduction from traditional fixed conceptions and criticism of the premises of legal reasoning with reference to the ends to be served was neglected. This will be looked into thoroughly in my third lecture. Second, the theory of law as a body of commands, as no more than a body of conscious products of the human will, has led law finders and lawmakers, both judicial and legislative, to overlook adjustment of precepts to the exigencies of human conduct and the demands of social progress. This, too, will be looked into in my third lecture.

Again, as we look from a functional standpoint at exclusive use of the method of the historical school, we may see two serious ill consequences. It led to taking the leading conceptions of the traditional law, given form by historical study, as necessary conceptions of all law and hence to opposing all change which did not conform to traditional historical lines as idealized. Also it led to taking accidents of legal history for necessary principles or necessary categories of universal law.

A striking example of how a historical accident could lead a great legal scholar and historian to a result at variance with common sense and the purpose of the law may be seen in Savigny's treatment of the doctrine of impossible and illegal conditions in testaments. The doctrine had its basis in *favor testamenti* in the beginnings of Roman law when the order of succession in the absence of a will was out of line with prevailing moral ideas. The reason for the doctrine ceased to exist centuries ago, and no other ground for it has remained than that it was laid down in the Roman law books. But a feeling that it was necessary to find some reason for what was to be found in the books led jurists to lay down a doctrinal distinction between the general intent and the particular intent of the testator which embarrassed the law for a time.

A number of striking examples were to be seen a generation ago at the time when the National Commission on Uniform State Laws was at work upon the uniform laws which have done much for a uniform commercial law. A well-known teacher of law in one of our leading law schools objected to departure from rules of the common law in order to make them "agree with business usages or even with what those usages were tending to become." Business usages should conform to historically settled principles, not the principles be adjusted to developing usages. An illuminating example, also, is insistence of historical jurists that the law of partnership must ignore the mercantile view that a partnership is an entity and follow the analogy of co-ownership with which the law began. Or, again, at a time when a majority of our jurisdictions had done away with separate courts of law and equity and separate equity procedure and we were coming to administer law and equity at the same time in one proceeding in the same case, one of our great teachers of law objected to "unwarranted assumption of equity powers by a court of law."

Such was the condition of the science of law at the end of the nineteenth century.

How we look at the science of law today will serve to introduce my second lecture.

TWO

Stare Decisis

THIRTY-SIX YEARS AGO, IN MY LECTURES ON INTERPRETATION of Legal History at the University of Cambridge, I said: "Law must be stable and yet it cannot stand still. Hence all the writing about law has struggled to reconcile the conflicting demands of the need of stability and the need of change. The social interest in the general security has led men to seek some fixed basis for an absolute ordering of human action whereby a firm and stable social order might be assured. But continual changes in the circumstances of social life demand continual new adjustments to the pressure of other social interests as well as to new modes of endangering security. Thus the legal order must be flexible as well as stable. It must be overhauled continually and refitted continually to the changes in the social life which it is to govern. If we seek principles, we must seek principles of change no less than principles of stability. Accordingly a chief problem to which legal thinkers have addressed themselves has been how to reconcile the idea of a fixed body of law, affording no scope for individual wilfulness, with the idea of change and growth and making of new law; how to unify the theory of law with the theory of making law and to unify the system of legal justice with the facts of administration of justice by magistrates."

Perhaps one may say of the legal order what Walt Whitman said of the universe:

. . . we are all onward, onward, slowly, bettering.
Life, Life is an endless march, an endless army (no halt but
    it is duly over).
The world, the race, the soul—in space and time the universe,
All bound as is befitting each—all surely going somewhere.

From time to time men have had a picture of a final, complete statement of the law which was to stand fast forever. But the most complete of them, the codification of Justinian, required supplementing and amendment in Justinian's lifetime, and the codification which bears the name of Napoleon is undergoing revision. The jurist's ideal law proves to be an ideal for time, place, and people, and the ideal shaped to time and place and people gives shape to his picture of a universal and eternal law.

What apparatus is there for making this continuous adjustment? There are two processes: lawmaking, the making of rules or authoritative establishing of principles by legislation, a political process; and law-finding, the ascertainment and formulation of principles by judicial decision in the common-law world and by juristic writing and teaching in the civil-law world.

In principles, starting points for judicial or juristic reasoning, we have to do with the reason element in law. Here we are in the domain of philosophy of law and it is important to review the available theories of that element as conceived today. Twentieth-century methods of jurisprudence are social philosophical, neo-realist, or sociological. The social philosophical jurists are or have been: neo-Kantian, neo-Hegelian, neo-idealists, or teachers of a revived natural law.

Taking them up in chronological order, we begin with the neo-Kantians, whose founder and leader was Rudolf

Stammler (1856-1938), professor at Halle and later at Berlin. He has been the chief single influence in philosophical jurisprudence in the present century. All that has been written on philosophy of law in the past fifty years shows his influence. Today the neo-Kantians are the dominant group. Stammler revived what the French jurists call juridical idealism, the search for ideals to which the law ought to conform. This had become discredited by the method of the metaphysical jurists in the nineteenth century, was not believed in by the historical jurists, who expected law to "just grow" like Topsy, and was ignored as irrelevant by the analytical jurists.

As achievements of the neo-Kantians we may note: (1) Change of front from the relation of ethics to particular abstract precepts to the relation of ethics to the administration of justice by means of legal precepts; (2) their theory of the social ideal as a controlling element in the judicial process; (3) adding a theory of just decision of cases to the theory of making just rules; (4) working out a theory of the application of legal precepts. Stammler substituted ideals of the claims involved in social life for the ideals of the abstract man *in vacuo*. He built his doctrine on Kant. But where Kant taught that the purpose of law was to reconcile the will of each with the will of all by a universal formula which would allow the greatest possible scope to each individual will, Stammler held that the purpose was to bring about a harmony of individual ends or purposes so that all possible ends of those who are legally bound are included.

Today there is a widening gap between the neo-Kantian right, represented by Giorgio Del Vecchio, retired professor at Rome, and the neo-Kantian left, represented by Hans Kelsen, professor in the University of California at Berkeley. The former thinks of law as a rule of life and man as both a moral and a social being. The latter connects with juristic realism and analytical jurisprudence as does the former with natural law.

The leading representative of the neo-Hegelians was Josef Kohler (1849-1919), professor at Berlin. He started from a proposition of Hegel that law is a phenomenon of civilization and sought to base a critique of law upon anthropology, comparative law, and comparative legal history, unified by history of civilization. He connects with the nineteenth-century historical school as Stammler does with the nineteenth-century philosophical jurists. Four points in his teaching are significant: (1) The theory of law as a product of the civilization of a people; (2) his theory of the relation of comparative legal history and the philosophy of law; (3) the theory of sociological interpretation and application of legal precepts, and (4) the method of formulating the jural postulates of the civilization of the time and place. Each of these makes a real advance in jurisprudence.

Hegel thought that law realized a simple idea of liberty. Kohler thought it realized a growing idea of civilization. The eighteenth-century ideal of an absolutely fixed, absolutely certain law was impossible of realization. Adjustment must be made to a constantly changing, and no doubt on the whole progressing, civilization. The task is to shape the law that has come down to us so as to further civilization.

Again, Kohler called for understanding of the social history of a people in its relation to law whereas the past had looked solely to political history. He sought an interpretation in terms of progressive development of human powers. Thinking of the law in terms of principles rather than of rules, he argued that the theory of ascertaining the will of the lawmaker, when applied to developing grounds of decision from a century-old code, was a fiction.

The surroundings of a codifier cannot interpret the section of a code as a statement of law as the surroundings of a testator can interpret a provision in a will. The codes in Continental Europe were to be interpreted not analytically nor historically exclusively, but sociologically.

What is most important, however, is Kohler's theory of formulating the jural postulates (i.e., the presuppositions) of the time and place as to what is right and just. Maintaining and furthering of civilization may be a measure of valuing interests, but it is too far from everyday problems of law to be a critique of doctrines and precepts. Kohler, to meet the need for a critique, would formulate, not the jural postulates of all civilization, but of the civilization of the time and place. I have found this theory very useful in treating the changing American law of liability to repair injuries incurred in the operation of industrial enterprises.

A recent group, conveniently called neo-idealists, have given us a logical, psychological relationist idealism. Chief among these is Gustav Radbruch (1878-1949). His discussion of the antinomies of justice is of particular importance. For example, in the law of liability to repair injuries in the operation of industrial enterprises, if we think only in terms of abstract justice, we may say no liability. If we think only of harmonizing interests as the end we may come to some such compromise as the last-clear-chance doctrine. If we think only of security we may adopt and develop the doctrine of *Rylands v. Fletcher*. Such problems are more complicated than the jurists of the past have assumed.

In France, in the nineteenth century following the Code (1804) while the law-of-nature philosophy remained for a time orthodox, there was little need of juristic activity. In the present century there came to be a notable revival of philosophy of law. It took two forms (1) a neo-scholastic social philosophy deriving from St. Thomas Aquinas, and (2) a positivist sociological natural law closely related to the mechanical sociology.

Leader in the first was François Gény (1861-1944) professor at Nancy, one of the outstanding figures in the science of law. His *Méthode d'interprétation* (1899, 2 ed. 1919) is best known. But his *Science et technique en droit privé positif* (4 vols. 1913-1924) is a full exposition and critique of philosophical jurisprudence. This book has not been appreciated as it deserves in the English-speaking world which, perhaps, has been repelled by an atmosphere of Thomistic orthodoxy which does not affect its intrinsic value. His recognizing the task of the jurist, as law finder and lawmaker, as one of finding starting points for legal reasoning, of choice from among competing starting points by a technique in the light of received ideals is a contribution of the first magnitude.

Leader of the other type of revived natural law was Leon Duguit (1859-1928), professor at Bordeaux. His primary field was constitutional law so that he approaches jurisprudence from the political rather than from the ethical side and essays to overhaul the whole content of law and resettle it on a scholastic-positivist basis. His system is one of natural law in that he holds that everything in law derives its validity from and is to be judged by a fundamental principle of right-and-law *(règle de droit)* of social interdependence through similarity of needs and diversity of functions. Following Comte, he holds that this fundamental precept is one reached by observation of social and economic phenomena and verified by further observation. But Duguit is important for public law more than for the law as a whole.

In the reign of historical jurisprudence interpretation of legal history became a subject of controversy and in the breaking away from the metaphysical philosophy of law a new philosophical direction was taken under positivist influence. For a time an economic interpretation of history and so likewise of legal history was in vogue. Out of this grew what Cardozo aptly called a school of neo-realists. It took two significant forms, psychological realism and skeptical realism. The former was a development of economic realism in the light of Freudian and behaviorist psychology. It conceived of the judicial process as shaped wholly and inexorably by psychological determinants of the behavior of the individual judge, quite ignoring the effect of a bench of judges upon judicial behavior, the constraint exercised by professional criticism and opinion, and what Maitland called the "toughness of a taught tradition." Out of this grew skeptical realism which rejected law in any other sense than the aggregate of items of judicial and administrative action. Law was what judges and administrative officials do, and what they do is law. There is skepticism as to the actuality or even possibility of objectivity in the judicial process. The leaders here have been the late Judge Frank (1889-1957) and Professor Karl N. Llewellyn of the University of Chicago. They have done a real service to our law in bringing home to bench and bar the need of thinking about the judicial process in action and seeking to improve its exercise. Professor Llewellyn laid out a useful program of study of this subject.

A group of Swedish realists have been developing a realist philosophy of law in the same direction, explaining psychologically law as an aggregate of independent imperatives establishing behavior patterns for those whom a lawmaking authority seeks to influence. They hold that rights and duties are imaginary. There is an imaginary bond originally derived from primitive magic. The reality is force applied by officials and the psychological basis of obedience which makes actual use of force unnecessary.

Study of the actual operation of the power of politically organized society in the administration of justice no less than the ethical principles on which it should proceed could be worth while.

Sociological jurisprudence became important in the present century. In the revival of philosophical jurisprudence some turned to positivism. Comte, the founder of sociology, was a mathematician and wrote when there was a tendency to take a mathematical-physical view of everything. Following the development of sociology, sociological jurisprudence went through a mechanical stage, a biological stage, and a psychological stage before coming to maturity. As it stands today, the sociological school has five characteristics. (1) It regards the working of the legal order, i.e., the body of authoritative guides to decision and of the judicial and administrative processes, rather than the abstract content of the authoritative precepts. (2) It regards law as a social institution, involving both finding by experience and conscious lawmaking, which may be improved by intelligent effort, and holds it the purpose of jurisprudence to make that intelligent effort. (3) It lays stress upon the social purposes which law subserves rather than upon sanctions. (4) It looks upon legal institutions and doctrines and precepts functionally, regarding the form of legal precepts as involving only a question of what is most adapted to the purposes of the legal order in the time and place. (5) It employs a pragmatist method which is consistent with different metaphysical starting points.

Sociological jurisprudence became significant when it attained after the beginning of the present century a stage of unification—first of unification of sociological methods and later of unification of the social sciences. A wholly detached, self-centered, self-sufficing science of law is inadequate. The legal order is a phase of social control. It cannot be understood unless taken in its whole setting among social phenomena.

Four jurists call for special notice in this connection. Mr. Justice Holmes (1841-1935) was at least the forerunner of sociological jurisprudence. He went through an analytical stage between 1870 and 1890, and a historical stage, as was to be expected in the latter part of the nineteenth century. But experience upon the bench and wide reading and deep reflection upon the juristic writing of the time led him at the end of the century to the sociological position. In understanding methods of judicial thinking and the scope and nature of legal logic, in understanding the relation between the law-finding element in judicial decision and the policies that must govern lawmaking, in conscious facing of the problem of harmonizing conflicting interests, in faith in the efficacy of effort to make the law effective for its ends, in a functional rather than anatomical point of view and in giving up the idea of jurisprudence as a separate science, he foreshadowed, if he did not always fully develop, the methods and ideas of a sociological science of law.

Eugen Ehrlich (1861-1922), professor at Czernowitz, endeavored to develop a technique of getting at the relation of customs of popular action to the law in the books and the judicial and administrative processes in action. He made a significant beginning of a sociological comparative law. There are a number of things that illustrate the importance of his studies of "living law" for everyday purposes of the science of law: the understanding of bankers when the legal theory and effect of letters of credit were in doubt, or the pressure by bankers on one of the principal banks in New York City not to plead *ultra vires* when sued on a supersedeas bond, or the understanding of the business world as to cancellation of orders, or the custom of collecting bank checks through the clearing-house when the courts had a rigid rule as to reasonable time.

Mr. Justice Cardozo (1870-1938) was perhaps at bottom a social utilitarian. But a twentieth-century social utilitarian had gone well beyond Jhering. His setting off of the judicial process from other meanings to which the term "law" had been applied and so obviating confusion between the regime, the process by which it is maintained, and the body of authoritative precepts by which it is governed or guided, has made much of the older discussion of the nature of law obsolete, and makes for a better understanding of this fundamental subject.

Leo Petrazycki (1867-1931), professor at St. Petersburg before the Russian Revolution and at Warsaw after 1918, gave us an intuitionist psychological sociology of law. His psychological theory of alternating stability and change is useful and the relation of his investigation of the process of motivation to recent neo-realist theories of law is manifest.

Comparing the science of law today with what it was at the end of the last century, we may say:

(1) It is functional, inquiring not only what law is and how it has come to be what it is, but what it does, how it does it, and how it may be made to do it better.

(2) It seeks team play with the other social sciences and so studies law in relation to the whole process of social control.

(3) It recognizes the importance of individualized application of precepts in adjudication as well as in administration and seeks to utilize instead of ignore the element of personal judgment and intuition derived from personal experience.

(4) It appreciates the problem of values, of a criterion of weighing interests or expectations, as one lying behind

the whole process of recognition, of delimiting and securing interests, of making or finding and shaping legal precepts, and applying them when made or found.

More particularly the sociological jurist of today insists upon five points: (1) Study of the actual social effects of legal institutions, legal precepts, and legal doctrines; (2) study of the means of making legal precepts effective in action; (3) psychological study of the judicial, administrative, legislative, and juristic processes as well as philosophical study of the ideals; (4) study not merely of how doctrines have evolved considered solely as legal materials, but study also of what social effects the doctrines of law have produced in the past and how they have produced them; and (5) recognition of individualized application of legal precepts—of reasonable and just solution of individual cases. This has been sacrificed in the past too often in the attempt to bring about an absolute certainty. There is need of study of systems of individualizing application. This involves study of the relations between the judicial and the administrative process.

Jurisprudence has now got well beyond the idea of a statute as the type of legal precept, of a legal precept as typically a rule, and of judicial law finding as a process to be treated on the analogy of legislation. This idea of the judicial process as one only of application of given rules of the strict law, rooted in the lay mind, is not without some lodgment in the professional mind also.

Going back to our starting point, the need of stability and the need of change—the need of stability is emphasized in the maxim *stare decisis et quieta non movere*. The materials with which it is maintained are to be found in the law reports.

Law finding through judicial decision is characteristic of the Anglo-American common law as finding by juristic writing is characteristic of the Continental civil law. It is at bottom the same process whether the immediate organ is judge or law teacher or writer. But it will be enough for present purposes to take it up as we know it in our law.

Common-law judges have sought to follow their own decisions, the decisions of their predecessors, and the solutions reached by others who administer the same system of law. It is important, therefore, for the practicing lawyer to know what has been decided and when and by whom. Hence in the beginnings of English law he took notes in court and passed his notes on to other lawyers and collected notes of cases from other lawyers. Also law teaching in England took on form in the beginning of arguing questions of law in the moots in the Inns of Court, and the notes of what the courts were deciding were the material from which arguments were drawn.

Beginning with notes taken by individual practitioners in open court and passing on and handing down of notes so taken, there come to be systematic private published reports of judicial decisions in the common-law courts. This is followed by private reporting in the courts of common-law jurisdictions in other parts of the world. In time there comes to be systematic public instead of private reporting, but private reporting goes on also along with annotation of and comment upon reported cases so that the literature of current case law has become enormous. Today judicial decision of certain special subjects begins to be increasingly regarded in the whole common-law world. Moreover, there is everywhere increasing interest in comparative law in which adjudication will probably play at least no less a part than juristic commentary and text writing.

When law has been found judicially what is its place in the legal order? Is it something to stand fixed and unchangeable, resisting all effort to replace or modify it until repealed or amended by legislation, or may the judicial process in the course of experience remake or replace it to respond to the needs of a changing world? It is to this question that the maxim is addressed.

The general proposition expressed in the maxim is that when a point of law has been decided by the highest court of a common-law jurisdiction it is of binding authority in all the courts of that jurisdiction, including the court which decided it, and is of more or less persuasive authority in other common-law jurisdictions, depending upon the standing of the court, the cogency of its reasoning, and the extent to which its conclusion fits into the general course of the law in the jurisdiction in which it is urged as persuasive authority.

Judicial decisions of the past and current judicial decisions are not the only materials of judicial law finding. Reason, analogy, ideals of justice, and general considerations of economic and political science enter into the apparatus which the court may employ.

To the neo-realist, individual intuitions, modes of thought, surroundings, and prejudices of the judges who are called upon to decide must also be taken into account and may prove controlling. But he puts too much stress upon the fact-finding basis of the law-finding activity. The facts come to the judge of the highest tribunal already found. He starts from them as given. With the facts given he has to (1) find the legal precept to be applied, (2) interpret it, and (3) apply it to the facts given. The process of finding the facts does not shape the process of finding the law. That has been done by someone else.

Theories of the judicial process must depend upon the aspect of that process to which they are directed. They may be directed to courts of first instance or to courts of review, which may make precedents, or to both, in which case their scope must be limited to the common element in each, namely, how to come to any decisions in any sort of controversy. Or they may be directed to the law-finding or law-declaring function of appellate courts or to the judicial process as a whole where one tribunal performs all the functions which are apportioned in modern administration of justice.

Huntington Cairns has given us an interesting discussion without perceiving that the four theories he considers are directed to different types of judicial process and that the one he adopts has application to only one of them. The four he takes up are those of Bacon, of Mr. Justice Cardozo, of myself, and of John Dewey. He adopts the last. Dewey's theory, which he approves, is applicable only to decisions by a judge of the first instance, sitting without a jury, to render judgment on the facts as he finds them. Bacon, who first essayed a theory of adjudication in the common-law world, sat at first instance in the Court of Chancery and as one of the judges in the Court of Star Chamber. At that time the law in each court was formative and he was concerned only with how far to be governed by such precedents as there were or by analogies from the law or by his personal judgment and discretion. Cardozo was considering the process of law finding in filling gaps in law in the sense of the body of recognized authoritative precepts in a matured developed system. Here the result must depend upon the relative value of the social interests to which the claims of the parties are referable. Clearly the process here must be governed by intuition gained by experience. In my own case, seeking to analyze the process of judicial law finding the facts being given, I said it involves finding the legal precept to be applied, interpreting the precept, and applying the precept to the facts given. Cairns considers that Cardozo is too elusive while I am too analytical. Dewey insists that the judge "does not first find the facts, then ascertain and develop the law and then apply the result to the facts."

But what he must do in the court of ultimate review today is to determine the law applicable and apply it to facts that come to him already found by someone else. Even at first instance, in an action at law the facts are found by verdict of a jury. In equity they are often found in the report of a master. At any rate in the appellate court, where alone the decision becomes a precedent, there is no process of finding both facts and law in one operation.

The notion that the judge (and this as to law finding by judicial decision must mean a bench of judges) decides the case after trying out different possibilities and then finds law and facts to the measure of his solution, may go for a justice of the peace. It is no picture of a state supreme court in action.

The law having been found by judicial decision, is it to stand as found until changed by legislation? Has the judicially found and declared rule such legislative authority that it must stand till repealed by enactment despite social and economic changes or changes in social, ethical, or economic thinking? That is the question raised by the maxim.

Three types may be distinguished among the American cases which have discussed the force and scope of the maxim. In one type the maxim is made to express a fundamental doctrine, in substance a rule, that a proposition of law established by judicial decision is only to be abrogated or altered by legislation. The older cases often put this in strong terms. Thus in *Palmer's Adm'rs. v. Mead,* 7 Conn. 149, 158 (1828), Hosmer, C. J., said: "There is not in the common law a maxim more eminently just, and promotive of the public convenience, than that of *stare decisis.*" He then quotes the respected eighteenth-century common-law authority, Sir William Jones, who had said "nothing is law that is not reason" was a dangerous maxim, and proceeded: "If law well established may be annulled by opinion a foundation is laid for the most restless instability. The decisions of one court may be overruled by another court, and those of the latter will only have a transient efficacy until some future court, dissatisfied with them, shall substitute new principles in their place. No system of inflexible adherence to established law can be as pernicious as such ceaseless and interminable fluctuations."

Today this view is not put in such downright and inflexible fashion but an example of what is widely held is: "The rule of *stare decisis* is entitled to the greatest respect and under our system of jurisprudence is an essential feature of the administration of justice. Where a decision, and especially a line of decisions, has been acquiesced in, where it has been followed in other cases, and has become a rule of property, and men have, in the conduct of affairs, learned to respect and conform to it, it becomes of especial and indeed of binding force, and should not be disturbed except by the interposition of legislative power." *Fuller v. Virginia Trust Co.*, 183 Va. 704, 712, 33 S.E. 2d 201, 205 (1945).

Insistence that correction can come only from the legislature persists in Massachusetts and Pennsylvania with respect to immunity of hospitals from liability for torts, although the case which established it was based on an English decision which had been repudiated in England when Massachusetts received it. The doctrine has been rejected by text writers, and given up by the majority of the jurisdictions which have passed upon it in recent years.

In a second type of case where courts have had before them a line of decisions long established which lays down a doctrine out of line with reason and with general and accepted principles of law, they have felt able to deal with the matter *de novo,* giving due weight to *stare decisis* but not feeling that remedy must be had by legislation. Of many cases of this type decided in the last century, it will be enough to quote from *Leavitt v. Morrow,* 6 Ohio St. 71, 80-81 (1856). The court said of a rule coming down from the seventeenth century and followed both in England and in America: "In the cases in which it has been followed, both in England and this country, it appears to have been adopted with little or no inquiry into the reason or justice of its application. The rule laid down is purely technical; and the reason assigned, that the stranger is not privy to the condition of the obligation, loses all its reality when we consider that the satisfaction must have been accepted by the plaintiff and assented to or ratified by the defendant. It would seem, therefore, that a rule which in its tendency is calculated to foster bad faith and defeat the purposes of justice ought not to be adhered to simply on account of its antiquity."

In a third type of case, a type responding to the legal order of today, it is recognized that it is a principle of social policy rather than an inflexible rule of law. This is well brought out in the opinion of Frankfurter, J., in *Helvering v. Hallock,* 309 U.S. 106, 119 (1939), and in *Park Construction Co. v. Independent School District,* 209 Minn. 182, 187, 296 N.W. 475, 478 (1941). In the latter case it is held that *stare decisis* is guiding policy, not inflexible rule. "It is no shield for plain error. Neither does it bar coordination of legal philosophy with that of new and commanding facts. Such coordination is necessary in order to satisfy the imperative demand for realistic judicial treatment of issues in their own actual environment rather than a synthetic one made from the materials of discarded doctrine."

It has long been recognized that *stare decisis* was primarily useful as a principle where rules of property and rules of commercial transactions were involved. But the law of private property no longer holds the compelling position it once enjoyed in philosophy of law. Even the conservative Supreme Court of Pennsylvania accepts judicial setting aside of "a rule of property long acquiesced in" for compelling reasons of public policy or the imperative demands of justice. *Smith v. Glen Alden Coal Co.,* 347 Pa. 290, 302, 32 A. 2d 227, 234 (1943). On the whole, experience of common-law courts with the maxim seems to show that if caution, good judgment, and sound reasoning are required of the law finder they are equally and no less required of the lawmaker. As a rule, the mistakes of the law finder have proved more easy to discover, rectify, and remedy than those of the lawmaker.

It may be worth while to go into some detail in looking into some problems of justice according to law which are arising today in order to be able to see how lawfinding is becoming aware of them, how it is treating them, and how far it is proving equal to them.

One problem in which notable progress has been going on is liability to repair injuries to life and limb. It is instructive to compare legislative treatment of this problem through workmen's compensation acts, which did away with doctrines and precepts that had grown up to the idea of fault, but substituted a body of rules affixing a definite detailed exact money award for each detailed injury. This is the method of rules of the strict law, comparable to the tariffs of composition for bodily injury in the Code of Hammurabi or the "for every nail a shilling" in the Laws of Ethelbert. Compare with this the juristic and judical working out of a principle of imposing upon an enterprise the burden of bearing the cost of repairing injuries inevitable in the course of operation and spreading the loss by including it in the price of its product. It should be noted that legislation left it to the courts to apply this principle in the Federal Employers' Liability Act.

Again when at the beginning of the present century the illness of Edward VII on the date when he was to be crowned and consequent unexpected postponement of the coronation procession created a new problem of relief from deprivation of an obligor, by unforeseen and unforeseeable circumstances, of a reasonably to be expected benefit from performance, the courts worked out a new principle of frustration, which has since called for much judicial application and is now treated in thirteen pages in the latest American treatment of the law of contracts.

Another significant juristic development is a doctrine of responsibilities to the public correlative to monopolies and immunities. There is an old and well settled concept of the common law of a public calling or public employment, calling for duties of public service, with special rules, principles, and standards applicable to them. Before the end of the Middle Ages the common law had established a legal category of public service with two basic requirements: a present necessity of maintaining an urgent social interest, and a condition of monopoly of the practical means of maintaining it. The principle, as we now see it, is one of satisfying so far as may be the reasonable expectations of mankind in society with a minimum of friction and waste. Developed further in the seventeenth century, this was taken up in the great case of *Munn v. Illinois,* 94 U.S. 113 (1876). It became settled that those who embarked their capital or directed their industry in what is a virtual monopoly in something of high public interest subjected themselves in that respect to legal regulation and were under the duties of a public calling. This is an outstanding achievement of judicial law finding.

Still another, in progress at the moment, is revival of the processes of discretion, dispensation, and mitigation, which had acquired a bad repute because of abuse under agencies of executive justice but are coming to be recognized as necessary instrumentalities in a complete system of justice and restored to their place in the judicial armory.

A well-known saying of Georgia's Chief Justice Bleckley may sum up what is to be said of *stare decisis*. When an error of the first magnitude moving in a wide orbit comes in conflict with truth and justice, "the maxim for a supreme court, supreme in the majesty of duty as well as in the majesty of power, is not *stare decisis* but *Fiat justitia ruat coelum.*" *Ellison v. Georgia R. R.*, 87 Ga. 691, 696, 13 S.E. 809, 810 (1891).

If, as many are telling us today, we are on the verge of what is to be a new age—the atomic age—it may be we shall need to try a new analogy for our way of putting the task of jurist and judge as law finders. Elsewhere I have spoken of the task as one of social engineering. "Engineering is thought of as a process, as an activity, not merely as a body of knowledge or as a fixed order of construction. It is a doing of things, not a serving as passive instruments through which mathematical formulas and mechanical laws realize themselves in the eternally appointed way. The engineer is judged by what he does. His work is judged by its adequacy to the purposes for which it is done, not by its conformity to some ideal form of a traditional plan. We are beginning in contrast with the last century, to think of jurist and judge and lawmaker in the same way. We are coming to study the legal order instead of debating as to the nature of law. We are thinking of interests, claims, demands, not of rights; of what we have to secure or satisfy, not exclusively of the institutions by which we have sought to secure or to satisfy them, as if those institutions were ultimate things existing for themselves. We are thinking of how far we do what is before us to be done, not merely of how we do it; of how the system works, not merely of its systematic perfection."

If a new age is impending, it will need social engineers upon the bench and in the law schools.

THREE

Reason and Reasoning
in Law Finding

"REASON," SAID COKE, THE ORACLE OF OUR LAW, "IS THE life of the law, nay the common law itself is nothing else but reason." But what did Coke mean by "reason"? He goes on to tell us that it "is to be understood of an artificial perfection of reason, gotten by long study, observation, and experience, and not of everyone's natural reason; for *nemo nascitur artifex.*" Earlier, when he was explaining to James I that although the court of King's Bench was said to be held before the king in person, yet he could not sit on the bench and decide cases because he was not learned in the laws of his realm of England "and causes which concern the life, or inheritance, or goods, or fortunes of his subjects, are not to be decided by natural reason, but by the artificial reason and judgment of law." *Prohibitions del Roy,* 12 Rep. 63, 65, 77 Eng. Rep. 1342 (K. B. 1608). When he came to explain this later he said: "This legall reason *est summa ratio* and therefore if all the reason that is dispersed into so many severall heads, were united into one, yet could he not make such a law as the law in *England* is; because by many successions of ages it hath beene fined and refined by an infinite number of grave and learned men, and by long experience growne to such

45

a perfection, for the government of this realme, as the old rule may be justly verified of it, *Neminem oportet esse sapientiorem legibus,* no man out of his private reason ought to be wiser than the law, which is the perfection of reason." *Co. Lit.* 97b (1621). What this means is that law is experience developed by reason and that without the experience which reason has applied to it a man's natural reason would not avail as a body of law.

Both reason and experience require definition, and *omnis definitio periculosa* was a wise maxim of the Roman law. Learning by observation of results in action how or how far legal precepts achieve practical results looked for is what Mr. Justice Holmes had in mind when he said "the life of the law has not been reason, it has been experience." But when we say experience is developed by reason what do we mean by reason? Not merely some logical method. The premises developed by formal logic may never have been tested for reasonableness. For example, the rational basis of *stare decisis* as an absolute fixed rule of decision, beyond reach of the courts and allowing only of legislative repeal or amendment of what has been judicially laid down in the decision of a litigated case in the highest court, is often put in terms of the rule itself.

Reason and reasoning are not the same thing. Reasoning does not as such necessarily lead to a reasonable result, nor is it necessarily guided by reason. Whether reasoning is reasonable depends on what it starts from, how it is carried on, and to what end. It is often mere association, superficial connection of one idea with another, without any real discussion and appraisal of essential points of connection.

Reasoning proceeds upon analogies. Too often inept analogies and inept applications of them are taken for reason. There is need of study of reasoning from analogies in the civil law, in the common law, and in the overhauling of law which is going on today.

It is instructive to turn to the exposition by General Fuller of the British army of the failure of commanders on both sides in the American Civil War to realize the change in relative value of rifle and bayonet and of the failure of commanders on both sides in the world wars of the present century to take account of what the Civil War in America could have taught them. If this was true in so intensely practical a subject as military science, it is perhaps no wonder that attention to the overwhelming importance of changed conditions upon established courses of legal reasoning has often escaped notice for so long in the science of law.

When I first began to read law books, some threescore years and ten ago, the books were still saying that pleading at common law was an application of formal logic. The declaration was a syllogism. The averments were to lead to the logical result formulated in the demand of judgment. Experience has taught us better. But it has been a long, painful, and expensive experience, and the lesson has not been learned fully as yet everywhere. We are still troubled in more than one place in the law by what I have been in the habit of calling the jurisprudence of conceptions—deduction by the method of the syllogism from fixed conceptions reached by the analogy of rules, institutions, and forms growing out of and expressing conditions of society in the past.

There has been too much abstract reasoning from attractive analogies of the past and not enough testing of those analogies in the light of how they meet or fail to meet the exigencies of reasonable expectations of men in the time and place. Abstract ethics and abstract politics must be supplemented by comparative study of the social

and economic conditions from which their abstract theories
are derived and of those to which they are to be applied.
This is the point to which the pragmatism of Holmes and
James is directed.

Let me take up ten cases, chosen from different parts of
the law, in which the administration of justice today is
struggling or has been struggling with analogies or fixed
conceptions which in their application, or in the application of deductions from them, defeat the purposes of administration of justice.

Procedural difficulties have obstructed the course of justice in all times. St. Paul's admonition "let all things be
done decently and in order" is easily taken to make order-
liness of procedure an end instead of a means toward the
true ends of a legal proceeding. An analogy which could
be used to bring about ordered procedure in the beginnings of law, and persisted for a long time in its consequences was the street fight in a village in a rural agricultural community and interposition of a magistrate to
stop the fight and preserve the peace.

In Roman law as late as the classical period, the second
century A.D., in a *legis actio,* an action of the strict law,
which had come down from the beginnings in the regal
period, the action was instituted by a dramatic representation of a fight in the street, command of the magistrate
to stop fighting, statements of what the fight was about,
and appointment of an impartial hearer to listen to each
side and decide the controversy. As Gaius, the Roman
Blackstone, tells the story, as still acted in his day in certain
cases, the plaintiff having summoned the defendant and
the defendant being in court, plaintiff and defendant
simulate each laying hands on the property in dispute.
Thereupon the magistrate says: *Mittete ambo*—"Let go,
both of you." Each then makes a formal claim of ownership and challenges the other to adjudication. Thereupon

the magistrate appointed a *judex* to determine the matter. The picture is one of a street fight, stopped by the magistrate, statement of the claim of each party to the ownership of a thing in dispute, and appointment of a judge of the question in dispute.

An action at law, then, was shaped originally to this picture. It was reduced to determination of a single simple point of fact asserted by one party and denied by the other, determination of that fact by the person appointed by law to make that determination, and a judgment according thereto. If all controversies which disturb the peace of a community could be disposed of in this simple way, the task of maintaining peace and order would be simplified and assured.

A controlling process in determination of controversies in the common-law system of administration of justice was pleading—the statement by each of the respective parties of what he contends is his case. But this became a highly technical process directed not to bringing out every fact or circumstance that each might have to urge in support of his case, but to the presentation of a single controversial issue, such as the one which provoked the street fight, a point of fact asserted by the one making his case and denied by the other. Hence the crucial thing in litigation was the issue. Blackstone tells us that issue, *exitus,* is the end, that is, the final purpose of pleading. In order to attain this purpose the statements of the parties must come to a single assertion of fact by one and denial thereof by the other. Thus as a result of complicated dexterous written fencing between counsel for the parties some one question could come to trial which would settle the controversy, perhaps as much as a test of the skill of the respective pleaders as of the merits of the dispute.

Bentham (died 1832) made a devastating attack upon the whole system of common-law pleading. A reform of it was attempted in England in 1834 and in New York in 1848, but neither went to the root of the matter. In England the system was radically changed in 1873 and the last remnants of the rules made to the street-fight analogy were done away with. In America a general movement in the same direction began in 1912, and since 1925 it has been becoming effective throughout the land. But it has taken one hundred and fifty years since Bentham wrote to rid the administration of justice of procedure shaped to the analogy of stopping the street fight.

Such is the tenacity of a tough tradition of scientific reasoning from an analogy long ago forgotten, that as short a time ago as 1906 an author whose writings were then widely read by students could say that the legal procedure in the United States was "the most refined and scientific system of procedure ever devised by the wit of man." James D. Andrews, 29 A.B.A. Rep. 56 (1906). Refined it certainly was. How far it was scientific depends on what is meant by science.

Another outworn analogy has long held back a law of torts adapted to the facts of life of today, namely, the analogy of an intentional attack by one man upon another with the simple weapons known to the beginnings of law. The old action of trespass *vi et armis* was made to the analogy upon which not only our law of torts but also a large part of our law of contracts took shape. The original writ in the action of trespass *vi et armis* recited an attack by one man upon another with swords, knives, and staves— a stabbing, cutting, or clubbing of one by another. All liability for wrong done to or injury suffered by another has been shaped by this analogy. How the analogy, already overworked, was made to serve also for what is practically the most important part of the law of contracts, will have to be taken up presently in another connection. At this point, it is enough to see how the analogy has been stretched to negligence, to injuries without fault due to escape or failure to control things or activities or agencies able and tending to escape or get out of control and do damage to person or property, and now, today, to imposing liability to repair injury to life and limb necessarily incident to the conduct of industrial enterprises or callings and hence to be reckoned as part of the cost thereof and taken account of in the fixing of rates and prices.

It is this last which has stretched the much-enduring analogy to the breaking point.

The stretching process began by invention of the action of trespass on the case. The particular facts were not something done with intent to injure by employment of swords, knives, and staves. But the facts of the case came to the same sort of injuries and the analogy was convenient in leading to a like result of liability to repair damage. It was not that the facts of the particular case appealed to the particular court at the particular time. The class of cases coming within the purview of trespass on the case was continuously extended by analogy, not case by case but category by category, unified by the unifying idea of a wrong. That idea as the sole ground of liability has been giving way.

A revealing case at one of the turning points of legal history, the beginning of the seventeenth century, must preface the story. The apprentices in the shops in London had organized "train bands," companies for training in military service. In a skirmish drill between two bands, the defendant accidentally discharged his musket and wounded the plaintiff, who brought an action of trespass for assault and battery. The defendant pleaded that the musket was discharged accidentally and by mischance with no intention to injure. The plaintiff demurred. There was judgment for the plaintiff. Where there was actual impact upon the body of the plaintiff the only defense could be justification by the order of an authorized superior or of an irresistible force. *Weaver v. Ward,* Hob. 134, 80 Eng. Rep. 284 (K. B. 1616). This was too much for the law-of-nature thinking of the seventeenth and eighteenth centuries and a way out was found through a moral theory of fault which got its classical formulation in article 1382 of the French Civil Code. Intentional injury to another was a fault. But so was also subjecting of another to an unreasonable risk of injury by acting without due care to prevent injury which a prudent person could reasonably foresee and guard against.

Liability without fault for acts of servants and agents had come down from a primitive household liability. It was reconciled with the fault theory by a fiction of representation. But it was so palpably strained that the New York Court of Appeals at first held a Workmen's Compensation Act unconstitutional as an arbitrary and unreasonable imposition of liability, and a minority of the Supreme Court of the United States so pronounced as late as 1919. But with the mechanizing of everything today, the maintaining and employing of instrumentalities of danger to life and limb have been leading us to feel that the losses which are now recognized as inevitably incidental to everyday operation of civilized life ought not to be imposed on the luckless individuals who chance to be hurt. We have learned how to spread the loss by requiring compulsory insurance.

A constantly growing category of liabilities where there has been no real fault, much less any intentional injury, is still for procedural reasons attributed to tort—literally wrongdoing. There is no suggestion of any element of aggression and in truth an element of wrongdoing is wholly absent. The use of a term which connotes wrongdoing still embarrasses a conspicuously living and growing part of the law.

We are not even now wholly emancipated from swords, knives, and staves. When we pass from the law of torts to the law of contracts we come upon them again.

Our law of contract has developed along two lines, one from the law of property, the other from the law of intentional injury. On the one hand the debtor who had borrowed his neighbor's horse under promise to return it next day, and the debtor who borrowed his neighbor's bag of gold or silver coin under like promise seemed to be depriving an owner of his property if he did not return the horse or the coins. Even if that promise was only to return the like value in money the duty looked like one to return property withheld without right, so that it seemed to raise questions of the law of property. On the other hand, one who could not be thought of as holding another's property which he ought to give up, but was doing a wrong in intentionally not performing a promise seemed to be a wrongdoer analogous to one who did wrong in some other way to another's injury, and so to be in the purview of trespass on the case. In a rural agricultural society of the beginning there was little in the way of what were thought of as business transactions to serve as analogy. Anything beyond policing had to be developed on the analogy of policing.

On the property analogy we got the action of debt for a liquidated sum of money formally acknowledged to be due by recognizance in open court or under the debtor's seal. On the tort analogy there was the action of *indebitatus assumpsit,* reciting the indebtedness existing and fictitiously acknowledged but remaining unpaid, or simple *assumpsit,* an informal undertaking to do or pay. In either case the theory was one of a wrong and the remedy was the appointed one for a wrong—trespass, but here trespass on the case.

In America today the formality of a private seal has

substantially disappeared and the attempt by a proposed uniform state law to keep the contract under seal alive came to nothing. We are driven to consider a very serious question as to the basis of what is called a simple contract, that is an informal promise, whether in writing or oral, to pay or perform.

On the whole, the progress of the law has been toward what had long been regarded as the moral position that promises as such ought to be kept. Demosthenes argued that laws should be obeyed because men as citizens had agreed to do so. Cicero in his treatise on duties emphasized the *prisca fides,* good faith in keeping promises, of the old Romans. A council of the early church in a pronouncement of Christian morals incorporated in the Corpus Juris Canonici laid down faithful keeping of promises as a tenet of Christian morals. The seventeenth-century jurists of the law-of-nature school repeated it as a proposition of natural law. Strykius said that we knew from Scripture that God held himself bound by a promise and that the devil and the Emperor were bound by promises also. The Declaration of Independence laid down that government derives its just powers from the consent of the governed who in effect consented to be bound.

The strict law was not concerned with morals. Its task was simply to preserve the peace. Property and intentional injury were the occasions of using swords, knives, and staves. The formal acknowledgment of indebtedness sufficed to meet the property analogy. What would bring a simple promise within the purview of the wrong analogy? This has been a question argued by jurists since the stage of natural law. Establishing of the genuineness of the promise has been suggested but has failed to meet the actual conditions of enforcement of law. More and more the law has been moving, and in the civil law world it has moved entirely, to complete accord with the precept of morals as laid down in a textbook taken as gospel when I was a student: "All social life presumes and rests upon the performance of promises or undertakings, declared or understood." 1 Parsons, *Contracts*, 3 (1853). We had been taking what seemed to be the last step in bringing the law of contracts into accord with the precept of morals in the recommendation of the English Law Revision Committee to do away with the requirement of consideration in a simple contract. But the movement has been at least arrested and we are told that the supposed moral foundation is illusory. The Marxian economic interpretation, the rise of the service state, and the theory of spreading the loss in liability for injuries are supposed to be leading to a radically different view of the significance of a promise.

But do we not get down ultimately to the expectations of men in civilized society, to the jural postulates or presuppositions as to what is just and right in civilized society? Can we divorce the law here wholly from ethics?

Is not one such presupposition a postulate that in civilized society men must be able to assume that those with whom they associate in the general intercourse of society will act in good faith, and as a corollary must be able to assume that they will carry out their undertakings according to the expectations which the moral sentiment of the community attaches to them? In consequence in a commercial and industrial society a claim or expectation that promises will be kept and undertakings be carried out in good faith, a social interest in the stability of promises as a social and economic interest becomes of the first importance. It requires that we secure the individual interest of the promisee, that is, his claim or demand to be secured in the expectation created.

It has been suggested that this approach is now superseded by the regime of state-prescribed contracts and favor to debtors in the social service state of today. It is true

that standard contracts, standard obligatory clauses in contracts, statutory and administrative prescribing of contract
provisions, and administrative control over making, performing, and enforcing of contracts have become everyday
matters. So also there is a tendency to insist (contrary to
the thinking in the last century) that the person bound to
perform keep faith to the last extreme even though it ruin
him and his family. Today it is insisted that the creditor
must take a certain risk of the debtor's ability to perform
and yet live a human existence. But there still is a great
field of everyday human business and general economic
activity untouched by the service state. So we come back to
the question whether reasonable expectations are created
by promises and are to be given effect or attach only to
promises in which there is some additional element to
which history has given the name of consideration.

This additional element is historically added to the will
to assume an obligation and grew out of the necessity in
the strict law of bringing enforceable agreements within
the analogy of property or of intentional wrong. The
analogy of creation or transfer of an estate in land was
met by the formal promise under seal. The analogy of a
trespass was met by "consideration."

Just what is meant by consideration has been a peren-
nial source of controversy since the seventeenth century.
It has been thought of and argued for as an equivalent for
the promise, as a moral ground of obligation, as detriment
to the promisee, as benefit to the promisor (whether past
or present, debated), and now, in its latest form, as requirement that the promise be part of a bargain. No wonder
that Ames spoke of the "mystery of consideration."

In the nineteenth century the metaphysical jurists, making everything turn on declared will to be bound, argued
for the safeguards of conveyance of property as called for
in contract also. But the informality of pioneer America

made a farce of the seal. In most of the United States there seemed to be no way of making a binding gratuitous promise. Accordingly the courts sought to find a way out by discovering some seventeen exceptions to the rule requiring consideration in a simple contract, most of which are now pretty well established. It would take a whole lecture to go into the details of these exceptions. It will be enough to say that they make use of such ideas as estoppel, waiver, gift, and special business devices for particular types of cases in order to get away from a disappearing historical requirement.

Holdsworth, after a critical historical review, pronounced "consideration" an anachronism. He said: "Our theory of contract is still governed by a doctrine which is historically developed, with great logical precision, from the procedural requirements of the form of action by which simple contracts were enforced." He added approval of Lord Mansfield's view, which in 1765 was too early for common sense to prevail over historical analogy, that consideration should be "treated, not as the sole test of the validity of a simple contract, but simply as a piece of evidence which proves its conclusion."

Parliament did not enact a statute abolishing the requirement. But Sir Courtney Ilbert reminds us that Parliament "is not interested in lawyer's law."

Recent English writers seek to salvage consideration by holding that the reality is bargain. The term "consideration" is only "the sign and symbol of bargain." What the law demands is a bargain. It will enforce a bargain but not a promise. Cheshire & Fifort, *Contract* 58 (4 ed. 1956). They consider there are two possibilities: To enforce any seriously made and proved promise or to enforce only those which are part of a transaction to which the promisee had contributed a material share. This is regarded as a fundamental doctrine of English law, differentiating it

from "foreign systems which enforce promises as such."
But English courts now enforce, as we have long been
doing in America, contracts for the benefit of third persons
not parties to the transaction. The advocates of the bargain
theory object to this as a departure from the settled English
doctrine. It gives up what differentiates English law from
the "foreign law" of the rest of the world.

Dickens has a useful word for this situation—"Podsnappery." Mr. Podsnap would wave behind him anything out
of the usual course of his business and dismiss it with the
conclusive judgment "not English." It is very well for
"foreign law" to shake off remnants of procedural shaping
of legal institutions of the economic order. Such things
are not for the law of England. The end of the reign of
swords, knives, and staves in the law of contracts may be
in Podsnappery.

But the law of contracts has not only suffered from a
bad analogy, but it has also furnished one for another
subject.

An important type of obligations may be called restitu-
tional. They have their rational basis in a corollary of the
jural postulate that in civilized society men must be able
to assume that those with whom they deal will act in good
faith. The corollary is that men must be able to assume
that others with whom they have dealings restore specifical-
ly or by equivalent what comes to them by mistake or
unanticipated situation whereby they receive at another's
expense what they could not reasonably have expected to
receive under the actual circumstances.

Gaius in the second century A.D. set off a catch-all
procedural category of obligations *ex variis causarum
figuris*. In the Institutes of Justinian (sixth century A.D.),
obligations neither contractual nor delictal are said to be
quasi ex contractu as analogous to those arising from contract. The French Civil Code in 1804 gave the situation

from which they arose the name of quasi contracts. Blackstone, seeing that the obligations to which they gave rise were sued upon in action of *indebitatus assumpsit,* an action in form upon a contract, called them contracts implied in law. The theoretical basis was a fiction of a promise implied in law used by the common law to allow recovery to prevent unjust enrichment of one person at the expense of another. This was justly criticized by Terry in 1884. Keener in 1893 took over the term "quasi contract" from the law books of the civil law. In 1937 the American Law Institute took the forward step of treating the obligation arising from unjust enrichment of one at the expense of another under the appropriate name of restitution. But as late as 1939 Sir William Holdsworth was unwilling to give up the term. "Contract implied in law and quasi contract is still in good usage." Paton, *Jurisprudence,* § 106 (2 ed. 1951). Thus restitution to prevent unjust enrichment was fixed and has more or less become fixed to the analogy of recovery upon an express promise.

What this has meant is illustrated by cases of unjust enrichment of corporations in *ultra vires* transactions. If a corporation cannot make a contract, how can it be held to have made the "implied contract" to restore what it holds? As the fiction of implied contract does not come labeled "fiction," as when John Doe sued as lessor of the plaintiff in ejectment, liability of a corporation in such cases made trouble. See Gray, J., in *Central Transp. Co. v. Pullman's Car Co.,* 139 U.S. 24, 60-61 (1891); *Sinclair v. Brougham* (1914) A.C. 398. Here the difficulty grew out of a false analogy.

Between a duty arising from an express promise one has power to make and a duty to make restitution for unjust enrichment, a duty not arising from any exercise of power, there can be no real relation.

Few subjects have made more trouble for the courts in recent years than causation. Judge Learned Hand wrote of the casuistic mysteries of causation. Dean Green said of causation that it did the work of Aladdin's lamp. Goodhart speaks of it as "a legal concept which cannot be defined in precise and accurate terms but must be described by a series of conflicting analogies." Harper and James write of the "little headway made in dispelling the confusion and taking some of the work load off of this weary concept." Sir Percy Winfield wrote that a "student who expects a scientific analysis of causation will be grievously disappointed. Up to a certain point the common law does touch upon metaphysics. But no test of remoteness of causation . . . would satisfy any metaphysician. On the other hand, no test suggested by metaphysicians would be of any practical use to lawyers." The difficulty is that, to fit the law to an analogy now wholly inapplicable to the task confronting the law of today, we have conjured up a pseudo-conception defying real definition or analysis. What American courts have said in attempt at definition takes up twenty-one double-column pages of volume 6 of Words and Phrases.

In causation we are confronted once more by our old friends "swords, knives, and staves." We first hear of it in *Earl of Shrewsbury's Case,* 9 Rep. 446, 77 Eng. Rep. 798 (K.B. 1610). This was the time when the case of the skirmish drill of the London train bands treated a case of negligent use of a firearm as if it were one of intentional aggression. The action was trespass *vi et armis* for disturbing the steward of certain manors in the exercise of his office. It was used in the sense of Aristotelian scholastic logic, which distinguished *causa causans* from *causa causati,* the causing cause from the cause of the effect. "Natural and proximate cause" came into the law books from one of Bacon's Maxims: *in jure non remota sed proxima causa spectatur.* But no one of the sixteen cases he discusses in support of his maxim had to do with negligence. The only one which might have relation to tort was one of fraud, as to which he says, "the rule faileth," and he adds that it "holdeth not in criminal acts."

Bacon's maxim was given currency by *Broom's Legal Maxims* (1845). Before that the cases speak of "consequential damages" in terms of Aristotle's distinction. In the celebrated squib case, *Scott v. Shepherd,* 2 W.Bl. 892, 96 Eng. Rep. 525 (C.P. 1773), the court said that the first wrongdoer should answer for all the damage that followed. In that case, as we should put it today, the one who first threw the lighted squib into the market house cast an unreasonable risk of injury on those inside, while those who impulsively threw it off their stalls had a privilege of self defense if the case was treated as one of intentional aggression. By the beginning of the nineteenth century the courts were still thinking in terms of assault and battery but were becoming conscious that it was an analogy, and a law of negligence was formative. The phrase "natural and proximate" came into use in *Ward v. Weeks,* 7 Bing. 211, 212, 131 Eng. Rep. 81, 82 (C. P. 1830). As the procedure of that time permitted joinder of defendants only where they had acted jointly, it became a question, in case of concurrent causation by independent negligences, of determining who was to be held.

At this point Broom's version of Bacon's maxim, in conjunction with what had been said in *Ward v. Weeks,* came into the picture. The maxim was first used in America in a case in Pennsylvania in 1863, *Scott v. Hunter,* 46 Pa. 192, but at that time the courts spoke of "natural and usual consequences." The current phrase "natural and probable consequences" comes from Cooley, *Torts,* 69-71 (1880).

It will have been seen that the maxim, as applied to

negligence, assumes a search for one person responsible, unless there was joint action or conduct; goes on the analogy of the named torts of intentional aggression; and so does not think of negligence, as we do today, as the imposing of an unreasonable risk of injury upon others and a threat to the general security, but as an attack on the person injured.

In the United States the subject of causation was critically looked into by Judge Jeremiah Smith in 1911-12. *Legal Cause in Actions of Tort,* 25 Harv. L. Rev. 103, 223, 303. He said: "To constitute such causal relation between defendant's tort and plaintiff's damage as will suffice to maintain an action of tort, the defendant's tort must have been a substantial factor in producing the damage complained of." Next Dean Leon Green put us on the right track by showing that what we must search for is the ambit of the risk created. This with a modern procedure which enables all those whose conduct contributed to the injury to be brought into one action, ought to be enough to deliver the law from the tangled condition to which the analogy of assault and battery had brought us.

But one more bad situation was created for a time by the use of the words "in the course of" and "arising out of" the injured employee's occupation, used in the Workmen's Compensation Acts. In the interpretation and application of these statutes the artificial niceties of causation were at first read into them and some of the resulting mischief still lingers in some spots in some jurisdictions.

Another analogy which is capable of doing and indeed has done no little mischief is one of which I had something to say at the outset, namely, the analogy of policing. It can be particularly mischievous in constitutional law. The function of politically organized society in the complex, crowded world of today is much more than one of policing.

The constitution is not a glorified police manual. Constitutional provisions lay down great principles to be applied as starting points for legal and political reasoning in the progress of society. A constitution may lay down hard and fast rules such as, for example, those fixing exact terms of office and apportioning duties among public functionaries. But the principles established by the constitution are not to be interpreted and applied strictly according to the literal meaning of words used by the framers as if they laid down rules. Interpretation of constitutional principles is a matter of reasoned application of rational precepts to conditions of time and place.

A principle gets the value as a starting point for legal reasoning from its possibility of fruitful application to actual conditions involved in litigation in the time and place. If it is limited, by its definition or by one imposed upon its interpretation, to exact meaning of words or conditions of fact which were current or existed or as they were understood when it was formulated, it loses its value for the purposes of a principle and becomes a rule. This defeats its end since a rule is fitted to precisely defined facts which may no longer obtain. Reason may be universal. But if the reasoning that is needed in order to apply the principle is tied to conditions which no longer exist nothing is left but idle and mischievous abstraction.

What may some day be regarded as the classical case of mistaken choice of an analogy in well settled common law for a new problem, raised by discovery of not previously encountered phenomena of nature, was furnished by the discovery of oil and gas and their use as fuel. It was assumed at once that ownership of the surface carried with it ownership of fuel materials beneath the surface, including gas and oil. When it appeared later that gas or oil might lie in something like a subterranean reservoir so that drilling by a neighbor might diminish or cut off flow from a previously drilled well, the courts had to find a principle on which to decide. The analogy was found at first in the doctrine of acquisition of ownership of wild animals by capture and reduction to possession. It was said that oil and gas were "minerals *ferae naturae.*" The court continued: "In common with animals, and unlike other minerals, they have the power and the tendency to escape without the volition of the owner. Their 'fugitive and wandering existence within the limits of a particular tract was uncertain,' as said by Chief Justice Agnew in *Brown v. Vandergrift*, 80 Pa. St. 147, 148. They belong to the owner of the land, and are part of it, so long as they are on or in it, and are subject to his control; but when they escape, and go into other land, or come under another's control, the title of the former owner is gone." *Westmoreland & Cambria Natural Gas Co. v. DeWitt*, 130 Pa. 235, 249, 18 A. 724, 725 (1889). But it turned out that there was not a simple question analogous to one between the owner of Blackacre and a trespasser who went on and shot a bird. Where, as it might be put, there is a subterranean reservoir of gas or oil below the surface, there is more to be taken into account than individual interests of substance of adjoining land owners who have drilled wells. There is also the social interest in the use and conservation of social resources. The analogy of the wild animal captured on his own land by the owner and the analogy of the wild animal taken by the trespasser have had to be given up.

A later principle, using the modern American doctrine as to percolating water, was set forth in *Ohio Oil Co. v. Indiana*, 177 U.S. 190 (1890). But it was not at once and generally taken up by the courts. It has had to be left to legislation, and text writers still talk about "the rule of capture." *Kulp, Oil and Gas Rights*, § 10.5 (1954).

One reason behind inept analogies from the past must

not be overlooked. Mr. Dooley said: "Hinnissy, I've the judicial timpermint. I hate worruk." It is easier to carry on reasoning from the analogy of a rule, maxim, or institution conveniently at hand in everyday law books than to study how far, if at all, they are related to the facts of today to which they are to be applied.

Those who would refer all law wholly to reason and scout experience should be cautious in identifying reason with reasoning from analogy.